COLLECTOR'S EDITION

The
OBAMAS

The White House Years

CONTENTS

JUNE 16, 2014, *Washington, D.C.*
President and First Lady Obama stroll from Marine
One on the South Lawn following a trip to California.

3

DECEMBER 10, 2013, *Johannesburg, South Africa*
The Commander in Chief moments before Nelson
Mandela's memorial service.

⸺∘INTRODUCTION ∘⸺

THE BEST YEARS OF OUR LIVES

ESSENCE's Editor-in-Chief looks at the real meaning of having the first African-American First Family in our hearts and minds, every day

The election of Barack Hussein Obama as the 44th President of the United States was a victorious march into history. For the first time, an African-American man would command the Oval Office, and global dignitaries would recognize him as the leader of the free world. Moreover, an African-American family over three generations would occupy the White House. In ESSENCE's September 2008 issue, the Obama family, then living in their South Side Chicago home, invited readers to get to know the then Illinois Senator; his statuesque wife, Michelle, who had balanced motherhood with a career as an attorney and hospital administrator; and their adorable daughters, Malia and Sasha.

"I know how blessed my girls are, because I know too many kids in my family and other communities whose futures are different because of one slip, one mess up, one thing that just didn't work out right," future First Lady Michelle Obama told writer Gwen Ifill at the time.

Over the next eight years much changed in our nation and the world—but since the Obamas made 1600 Pennsylvania Avenue their home, what has not changed is the family's commitment to the intrinsic value of goodness, their loyalty and service to country, and their ability to reach for the sky while keeping their feet firmly planted on the ground.

Ever since the Obamas took up residence at 1600 Pennsylvania Avenue, we have chronicled their extraordinary journey. Beginning with *The Obamas:*

Portrait of America's New First Family (2009), through *The Obamas in The White House* (2009) and *A Salute to Michelle Obama* (2013), our goal has been to pull back the lens and highlight those milestones of the President's and his family's time in the White House that meant the most to you.

Now, in *The Obamas: The White House Years,* ESSENCE is pleased to present a commemorative look at significant and seminal moments during the Obamas' tenure. From their two inaugurations, international travels and state dinners to day-to-day encounters with everyday citizens, *The Obamas* showcases images that offer intimacy and empowerment to ESSENCE readers.

We've divided the book into three sections focusing on President Obama, First Lady Michelle Obama, and the Obamas as a family. It's all here—the historic moments, the invite-only events, the interactions with extraordinary everyday people and world leaders, the couple's individual initiatives aimed at strengthening families and communities, and the blossoming of two future leaders—Malia and Sasha—before our very eyes.

The Obamas have earned a special place in our hearts and in our homes. Looking back at every great moment—spectacular and intimate—you will appreciate why we will forever celebrate this once-in-a-lifetime moment for our nation and the world.

Vanessa K. De Luca

VANESSA K. DE LUCA
Editor-in-Chief

2008, *Washington, D.C.*
A focused Obama ready to take flight
during his first presidential campaign

CHAPTER ONE

PRESIDENT BARACK HUSSEIN OBAMA

On November 4, 2008, Senator Obama was elected as the 44th President of the United States. Over the next eight years, he would transform our nation and transfix millions of supporters.

JUNE 26, 2015, *Charleston, SC*
While delivering a gut-wrenching eulogy,
Obama belts out the spiritual "Amazing Grace."

———∘ REMEMBRANCE ∘———

"AMAZING GRACE"

On June 26, 2015, President Obama eulogized the Honorable Reverend Clementa C. Pinckney, pastor of Mother Emanuel African Methodist Episcopal Church. Pinckney was one of nine parishioners murdered in their church home. Within those storied walls, President Obama delivered his most significant speech during his leadership tenure.

Giving all praise and honor to God. The Bible calls us to hope. To persevere, and have faith in things not seen. [*Applause.*]

"They were still living by faith when they died," Scripture tells us. "They did not receive the things promised; they only saw them and welcomed them from a distance, admitting that they were foreigners and strangers on Earth."

We are here today to remember a man of God who lived by faith. A man who believed in things not seen. A man who believed there were better days ahead, off in the distance. A man of service who persevered, knowing full well he would not receive all those things he was promised, because he believed his efforts would deliver a better life for those who followed.

To Jennifer, his beloved wife; to Eliana and Malana, his beautiful, wonderful daughters; to the Mother Emanuel family and the people of Charleston, the people of South Carolina.

I cannot claim to have the good fortune to know Reverend Pinckney well. But I did have the pleasure of knowing him and meeting him here in South Carolina, back when we were both a little bit younger. [*Laughter.*] Back when I didn't have visible grey hair. [*Laughter.*] The first thing I noticed was his graciousness, his smile, his reassuring baritone, his deceptive sense of humor—all qualities that helped him wear so effortlessly a heavy burden of expectation.

Friends of his remarked this week that when Clementa Pinckney entered a room, it was like the future arrived; that even from a young age, folks knew he was special. Anointed. He was the progeny of a long line of the faithful—a family of preachers who spread God's word, a family of protesters who sowed change to expand voting rights and desegregate the South. Clem heard their instruction, and he did not forsake their teaching.

He was in the pulpit by 13, pastor by 18, public servant by 23. He did not exhibit any of the cockiness of youth, nor youth's insecurities; instead, he set an example worthy of his position, wise beyond his years, in his speech, in his conduct, in his love, faith, and purity.

As a senator, he represented a sprawling swath of the Lowcountry, a place that has long been one of the most neglected in America. A place still wracked by poverty and inadequate schools; a place where children can still go hungry and the sick can go without treatment. A place that needed somebody like Clem. [*Applause.*]

His position in the minority party meant the odds of winning more resources for his constituents were often long. His calls for greater equity were too often unheeded; the votes he cast were sometimes lonely. But he never gave up. He stayed true to his convictions. He would not grow discouraged. After a full day at the capitol, he'd climb into his car and head to the church to draw sustenance from his family, from his ministry, from the community that loved and needed him. There he would fortify his faith and imagine what might be.

Reverend Pinckney embodied a politics that was neither mean nor small. He conducted himself quietly, and kindly, and diligently. He encouraged progress not by pushing his ideas alone, but by seeking out your ideas, partnering with you to make things happen. He was full of empathy and fellow feeling, able to walk in somebody else's shoes and see through their eyes. No wonder one of his senate colleagues remembered Senator Pinckney as "the most gentle of the 46 of us—the best of the 46 of us."

Clem was often asked why he chose to be a pastor and a public servant. But the person who asked probably didn't know the history of the AME church. [*Applause.*] As our brothers and sisters in the AME church know, we don't make those distinctions. "Our calling," Clem once said, "is not just within the walls of the congregation, but...the life and community in which our congregation resides." [*Applause.*]

He embodied the idea that our Christian faith demands deeds and not just words; that the "sweet hour of prayer" actually lasts the whole week long [*applause*]; that to put our faith in action is more than individual salvation, it's about our collective salvation; that to feed the hungry and clothe the naked and house the homeless is not just a call for isolated charity but the imperative of a just society.

What a good man. Sometimes I think that's the best thing to hope for when you're eulogized—after all the words and recitations and resumes are read, to just say someone was a good man. [*Applause.*]

> ## To settle for symbolic gestures without following up with the hard work of more lasting change—that's how we lose our way again."
> **—PRESIDENT OBAMA**

You don't have to be of high station to be a good man. Preacher by 13. Pastor by 18. Public servant by 23. What a life Clementa Pinckney lived. What an example he set. What a model for his faith. And then to lose him at 41—slain in his sanctuary with eight wonderful members of his flock, each at different stages in life but bound together by a common commitment to God.

Cynthia Hurd. Susie Jackson. Ethel Lance. DePayne Middleton-Doctor. Tywanza Sanders. Daniel L. Simmons. Sharonda Coleman-Singleton. Myra Thompson. Good people. Decent people. God-fearing people. [*Applause.*] People so full of life and so full of kindness. People who ran the race, who persevered. People of great faith.

To the families of the fallen, the nation shares in your grief. Our pain cuts that much deeper because it happened in a church. The church is and always has been the center of African-American life [*applause*], a place to call our own in a too often hostile world, a sanctuary from so many hardships.

Over the course of centuries, black churches served as "hush harbors" where slaves could worship in safety; praise houses where their free descendants could gather and shout hallelujah [*applause*]; rest stops for the weary along the Underground Railroad; bunkers for the foot soldiers of the Civil Rights Movement. They have been, and continue to be, community centers where we organize for jobs and justice; places of scholarship and network; places where children are loved and fed and kept out of harm's way, and told that they are beautiful and smart [*applause*] and taught that they matter. [*Applause.*] That's what happens in church.

That's what the black church means. Our beating heart. The place where our dignity as a people is inviolate. When there's no better example of this tradition than Mother Emanuel [*applause*]—a church built by blacks seeking liberty, burned to the ground because its founder sought to end slavery, only to rise up again, a Phoenix from these ashes. [*Applause.*]

When there were laws banning all-black church gatherings, services happened here anyway, in defiance of unjust laws. When there was a righteous movement to dismantle Jim Crow, Dr. Martin Luther King, Jr. preached from its pulpit, and marches began from its steps. A sacred place, this church. Not just for

JUNE 26, 2015, *Charleston, SC*
The President embraces grieving
family members of the Charleston 9.

FEBRUARY 5, 2009, *Camp Springs, MD*
President Barack Obama on his first flight aboard
Air Force One, at Andrews Air Force Base.

JUNE 19, 2011, *Washington, D.C.*
POTUS welcoming patrons at a local ice
cream parlor during a Father's Day outing.

MAY 1, 2011, *Washington, D.C.*
The President with the national security team receiving
an update on the mission against Osama bin Laden.

APRIL 18, 2012, *Dearborn, MI*
While aboard the now infamous Rosa
Parks bus, the President reflects.

FEBRUARY 18, 2016, *Washington, D.C.*
The Obamas welcome 106-year-old Virginia
McLaurin to a Black History Month reception.

OCTOBER 14, 2011, *Washington, D.C.*
Living the Dream: President Obama tours the
Martin Luther King, Jr., National Memorial.

JANUARY 28, 2013, *Washington, D.C.*
Always focused, the President takes a meeting
in the Roosevelt Room of the White House.

*People of goodwill will
continue to debate the
merits of various policies,
as our democracy
requires—this is a big,
raucous place, America is."*
—PRESIDENT OBAMA

AUGUST 31, 2012, *El Paso, TX*
POTUS delivering remarks to troops following their Iraq combat mission.

18

" *For too long, we've been blind to the way past injustices shape the present. Perhaps we see that now.*" —PRESIDENT OBAMA

> *If we can find that grace, anything is possible. If we can tap that grace, everything can change."*
> —PRESIDENT OBAMA

AUGUST 12, 2009, *Washington, D.C.*
President Obama shares a moment with Presidential Medal of Freedom recipient Sidney Poitier.

MAY 19, 2013, *Atlanta*
Dr. John Wilson, Jr., presents President Obama with an honorary Doctor of Laws degree at
Morehouse College.

JANUARY 14, 2014, *Washington, D.C.*
The President gives basketball tips to NBA All-Stars Dwyane Wade (left) and LeBron James (right)
in the East Room of the White House.

JANUARY 13, 2012, *Washington, D.C.*
A Meeting of Heroes: President Obama with the legendary Tuskegee Airmen in the East Garden Room of the White House.

blacks, not just for Christians, but for every American who cares about the steady expansion [*applause*] of human rights and human dignity in this country; a foundation stone for liberty and justice for all. That's what the church meant. [*Applause.*]

We do not know whether the killer of Reverend Pinckney and eight others knew all of this history. But he surely sensed the meaning of his violent act. It was an act that drew on a long history of bombs and arson and shots fired at churches—not random, but as a means of control, a way to terrorize and oppress. [*Applause.*] An act that he imagined would incite fear and recrimination, violence and suspicion. An act that he presumed would deepen divisions that trace back to our nation's original sin.

Oh, but God works in mysterious ways. [*Applause.*] God has different ideas. [*Applause.*]

He didn't know he was being used by God. [*Applause.*] Blinded by hatred, the alleged killer could not see the grace surrounding Reverend Pinckney and that Bible-study group—the light of love that shone as they opened the church doors and invited a stranger to join in their prayer circle. The alleged killer could have never anticipated the way the families of the fallen would respond when they saw him in court—in the midst of unspeakable grief, with words of forgiveness. He couldn't imagine that. [*Applause.*]

The alleged killer could not imagine how the city of Charleston, under the good and wise leadership of Mayor Riley [*applause*]— how the state of South Carolina, how the United States of America would respond: not merely with revulsion at his evil act, but with big-hearted generosity and, more importantly, with a thoughtful introspection and self-examination that we so rarely see in public life.

Blinded by hatred, he failed to comprehend what Reverend Pinckney so well understood: the power of God's grace. [*Applause.*]

This whole week, I've been reflecting on this idea of grace. [*Applause.*] The grace of the families who lost loved ones. The grace that Reverend Pinckney would preach about in his sermons. The grace described in one of my favorite hymns—the one we all know: Amazing grace, how sweet the sound that saved a wretch like me. [*Applause.*] I once was lost, but now I'm found; was blind but now I see. [*Applause.*]

According to the Christian tradition, grace is not earned. Grace is not merited. It's not something we deserve. Rather, grace is the free and benevolent favor of God [*applause*]— as manifested in the salvation of sinners and the bestowal of blessings. Grace.

As a nation, out of this terrible tragedy, God has visited grace upon us, for he has allowed us to see where we've been blind. [*Applause.*] He has given us the chance, where we've been lost, to find our best selves. [*Applause.*] We may not have earned it, this grace, with our rancor and complacency, and short-sightedness and fear of each other—but we got it all the same. He gave it to us anyway. He's once more given us grace. But it is up to us now

That's what I've felt this week—an open heart. That, more than any particular policy or analysis, is what's called upon right now."

—PRESIDENT OBAMA

MARCH 15, 2009, *Washington, D.C.*
The Obama family dog, Bo, joins
Mr. President for a quick jog .

God has visited grace upon us, for he has allowed us to see where we've been blind."
—PRESIDENT OBAMA

24

AUGUST 26, 2013, *Washington, D.C.*
Faith leaders and the President pray in the
Oval Office while meeting to discuss the 50th
anniversary of the March on Washington.

It would be a refutation of the forgiveness expressed by those families if we merely slipped into old habits."
—PRESIDENT OBAMA

FEBRUARY 27, 2015, *Washington, D.C.*
My Brother's Keeper mentees gather for
lunch with the President in the White House.

"A roadway toward a better world. He knew that the path of grace involves an open mind—but, more importantly, an open heart."
—PRESIDENT OBAMA

MAY 24, 2011, *London, England*
The President joins Queen Elizabeth II
for dinner during a State Banquet at
Buckingham Palace.

JANUARY 20, 2009, *Washington, D.C.*
Mr. Obama showing off his new Presidential swag, after a long day that included attending ten inaugural balls and being sworn in as Commander in Chief.

MAY 19, 2010, *Washington, D.C.*
President Barack Obama, First Lady Michelle Obama, President Felipe Calderón of Mexico, and his wife, Mrs. Margarita Zavala, ride a trolley to a tent on the South Lawn of the White House for the State Dinner reception.

None of us can or should expect a transformation in race relations overnight."
—PRESIDENT OBAMA

MARCH 14, 2012, *Washington, D.C.*
The President enjoys a funny moment
during a State Dinner on the South Lawn.

66

Grace is not earned.
Grace is not merited. It's
not something we deserve."
—PRESIDENT OBAMA

MARCH 10, 2016, *Washington, D.C.*
The Obamas are joined by Canadian
Prime Minister Justin Trudeau and his
wife, Sophie Grégoire Trudeau, during a
State Dinner at the White House.

JULY 24, 2015, *Nairobi, Kenya*
The President enjoys a homecoming celebration with family, including half-sister Auma Obama (in white).

MAY 8, 2009, *Washington, D.C.*
Does your hair feel like mine? The President compares haircuts with a staffer's son while in the Oval Office.

DECEMBER 10, 2013, *Johannesburg, South Africa* Graça Machel, widow of late South African President Nelson Mandela, talks with President Obama at a memorial service for her husband.

MARCH 20, 2016, *Havana, Cuba*
The Obamas arrive in Cuba for a historic visit, the first of any sitting U.S. President in nearly 100 years.

MARCH 21, 2016, *Havana, Cuba*
President Obama with Salvador Valdés
Mesa (left), Vice President of the
Council of State, in Revolution Square.

to make the most of it, to receive it with gratitude, and to prove ourselves worthy of this gift.

For too long, we were blind to the pain that the Confederate flag stirred in too many of our citizens. [*Applause.*] It's true, a flag did not cause these murders. But as people from all walks of life, Republicans and Democrats, now acknowledge—including Governor Haley, whose recent eloquence on the subject is worthy of praise [*applause*]—as we all have to acknowledge, the flag has always represented more than just ancestral pride. [*Applause.*] For many, black and white, that flag was a reminder of systemic oppression and racial subjugation. We see that now.

Removing the flag from this state's capitol would not be an act of political correctness; it would not be an insult to the valor of Confederate soldiers. It would simply be an acknowledgment that the cause for which they fought—the cause of slavery—was wrong [*applause*]; the imposition of Jim Crow after the Civil War, the resistance to civil rights for all people, was wrong. [*Applause.*] It would be one step in an honest accounting of America's history, a modest but meaningful balm for so many unhealed wounds. It would be an expression of the amazing changes that have transformed this state and this country for the better, because of the work of so many people of goodwill, people of all races striving to form a more perfect union. By taking down that flag, we express God's grace. [*Applause.*]

But I don't think God wants us to stop there. [*Applause.*] For too long, we've been blind to the way past injustices continue to shape the present. Perhaps we see that now. Perhaps this tragedy causes us to ask some tough questions about how we can permit so many of our children to languish in poverty, or attend dilapidated schools, or grow up without prospects for a job or for a career. [*Applause.*]

Perhaps it causes us to examine what we're doing to cause some of our children to hate. [*Applause.*] Perhaps it softens hearts towards those lost young men, tens and tens of thousands caught up in the criminal justice system [*applause*]—and leads us to make sure that that system is not infected with bias; that we embrace changes in how we train and equip our police so that the bonds of trust between law enforcement and the communities they serve make us all safer and more secure. [*Applause.*]

> **"** *He was full of empathy and fellow feeling, able to walk in somebody else's shoes and see through their eyes.* **"**
> **—PRESIDENT OBAMA**

Maybe we now realize the way racial bias can infect us even when we don't realize it, so that we're guarding against not just racial slurs, but we're also guarding against the subtle impulse to call Johnny back for a job interview but not Jamal. [*Applause.*] So that we search our hearts when we consider laws to make it harder for some of our fellow citizens to vote. [*Applause.*] By recognizing our common humanity, by treating every child as important, regardless of the color of their skin or the station into which they were born, and to do what's necessary to make opportunity real for every American—by doing that, we express God's grace. [*Applause.*]

For too long—
AUDIENCE: For too long!
THE PRESIDENT: For too long, we've been blind to the unique mayhem that gun violence inflicts upon this nation. [*Applause.*] Sporadically, our eyes are open: When eight of our brothers and sisters are cut down in a church basement, 12 in a movie theater, 26 in an elementary school. But I hope we also see the 30 precious lives cut short by gun violence in this country every single day; the countless more whose lives are forever changed—the survivors crippled, the children traumatized and fearful every day as they walk to school, the husband who will never feel his wife's warm touch, the entire communities whose grief overflows every time they have to watch what happened to them happen to some other place.

The vast majority of Americans—the majority of gun owners—want to do something about this. We see that now. [*Applause.*] And I'm convinced that by acknowledging the pain and loss of others, even as we respect the traditions and ways of life that make up this beloved country—by making the moral choice to change, we express God's grace. [*Applause.*]

We don't earn grace. We're all sinners. We don't deserve it. [*Applause.*] But God gives it to us anyway. [*Applause.*] And we choose how to receive it. It's our decision how to honor it.

None of us can or should expect a transformation in race relations overnight. Every time something like this happens, somebody says we have to have a conversation about race. We talk a lot about race. There's no shortcut. And we don't need more talk. [*Applause.*] None of us should believe that a handful of gun safety measures will prevent every tragedy. It will not. People of goodwill will continue to debate the merits of various

JULY 11, 2009, *Cape Coast, Ghana*
The Obama family during an emotional
visit to "The Door of No Return," a former
holding place for enslaved Africans.

policies, as our democracy requires—this is a big, raucous place, America is. And there are good people on both sides of these debates. Whatever solutions we find will necessarily be incomplete.

But it would be a betrayal of everything Reverend Pinckney stood for, I believe, if we allowed ourselves to slip into a comfortable silence again. [*Applause.*] Once the eulogies have been delivered, once the TV cameras move on, to go back to business as usual—that's what we so often do to avoid uncomfortable truths about the prejudice that still infects our society. [*Applause.*] To settle for symbolic gestures without following up with the hard work of more lasting change—that's how we lose our way again.

It would be a refutation of the forgiveness expressed by those families if we merely slipped into old habits, whereby those who disagree with us are not merely wrong but bad; where we shout instead of listen; where we barricade ourselves behind preconceived notions or well-practiced cynicism.

Reverend Pinckney once said, "Across the South, we have a deep appreciation of history—we haven't always had a deep appreciation of each other's history." [*Applause.*] What is true in the South is true for America. Clem understood that justice grows out of recognition of ourselves in each other. That my liberty depends on you being free, too. [*Applause.*] That history can't be a sword to justify injustice, or a shield against progress, but must be a manual for how to avoid repeating the mistakes of the past—how to break the cycle. A roadway toward a better world. He knew that the path of grace involves an open mind—but, more importantly, an open heart.

JUNE 27, 2013, *Dakar, Senegal*
The Obamas arriving at an official
dinner at the Presidential Palace.

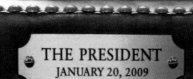

THE PRESIDENT
JANUARY 20, 2009

"

*The Bible calls us to hope.
To persevere, and have
faith in things not seen."*

—PRESIDENT OBAMA

That's what I've felt this week—an open heart. That, more than any particular policy or analysis, is what's called upon right now, I think—what a friend of mine, the writer Marilynne Robinson, calls "that reservoir of goodness, beyond, and of another kind, that we are able to do each other in the ordinary cause of things."

That reservoir of goodness. If we can find that grace, anything is possible. [*Applause.*] If we can tap that grace, everything can change. [*Applause.*]

Amazing grace. Amazing grace.

[*Begins to sing*] Amazing grace [*applause*]—how sweet the sound, that saved a wretch like me; I once was lost, but now I'm found; was blind but now I see. [*Applause.*]

Clementa Pinckney found that grace.

Cynthia Hurd found that grace.

Susie Jackson found that grace.

Ethel Lance found that grace.

DePayne Middleton-Doctor found that grace.

Tywanza Sanders found that grace.

Daniel L. Simmons, Sr., found that grace.

Sharonda Coleman-Singleton found that grace.

Myra Thompson found that grace.

Through the example of their lives, they've now passed it on to us. May we find ourselves worthy of that precious and extraordinary gift, as long as our lives endure. May grace now lead them home. May God continue to shed His grace on the United States of America. [*Applause.*]

JULY 26, 2012, *Washington, D.C.*
The Commander in Chief leads a meeting in the Cabinet Room of the White House.

JANUARY 12, 2016, *Washington, D.C.*
President Barack Obama walks through
the West Colonnade before delivering his
final State of the Union address.

That's what the black church means. Our beating heart. The place where our dignity as a people is inviolate."
—PRESIDENT OBAMA

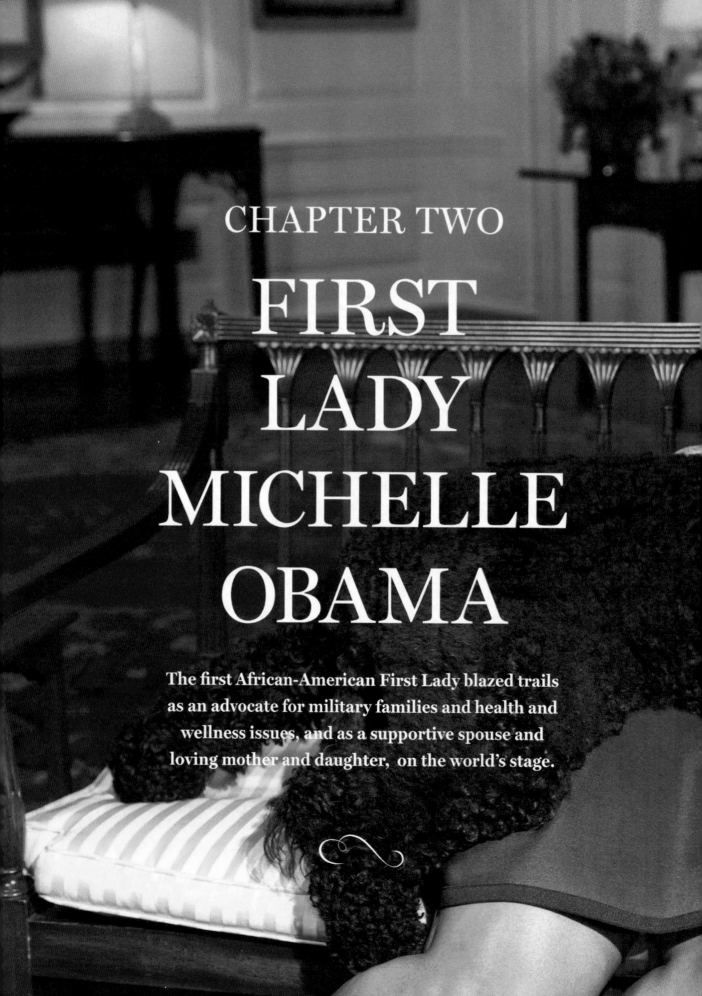

CHAPTER TWO
FIRST LADY MICHELLE OBAMA

The first African-American First Lady blazed trails as an advocate for military families and health and wellness issues, and as a supportive spouse and loving mother and daughter, on the world's stage.

APRIL 14, 2014, *Washington, D.C.*
First Lady Michelle Obama hugs
family pets Sunny and Bo during a
videotaping in the White House.

SEPTEMBER 17, 2014, *Memphis*
First Lady Michelle Obama talks with 10-year-old patient
Courtney Davis before Davis introduces the First Lady to
other patients at St. Jude Children's Research Hospital.

———◦ ESSAY ◦———

BE FEARLESS

I learned a long time ago that when you've had some success, it's not enough to just sit back and enjoy it. You've got to reach back and pull someone else up too.

I keep that lesson with me every day, whether it's as the First Lady, as a woman or as a mom. I tell my girls all the time that they are beautiful, that they are smart and that they should live life without fear of failing. I say these things because they are absolutely true and because I want to make sure they hear these words as often as possible. They deserve it. And I hope they believe it.

For 40 years now, ESSENCE magazine has given us that same encouragement. Each issue tells Black women that we are beautiful. We are smart. We are strong. Our opinions matter. We should be fearless.

ESSENCE is a community of support and a source of inspiration. Here we can be proud of ourselves and proud of one another. Here we see our contributions and our potential. We can take comfort in how far we've come and have confidence in where we're headed. In 40 years we've gone from the shadows of our civil rights victories to leading the way as business owners, professors, scientists, artists and entrepreneurs. With each step, this magazine has shown us who we are and what we can be.

And we need to keep it up. I have met many women—some older, some younger—who do not have someone in their lives who tells them they're good enough, that they should dream big dreams, that their hard work will pay off.

This is why I started the White House leadership and mentoring initiative and have organized mentoring events around the country. I want to help young people see their potential, to be confident in using their voices, to own the power of their experiences and to recognize that they have an important role to play in the life of this country.

With the mentoring program in D.C., we've paired local high school girls with women on the White House staff, who spend time with them each month. The women listen to their concerns, provide some guidance when asked, expose the young girls to new ways of thinking, discuss their future and, perhaps most important, demonstrate that they were once just like them.

Each young woman has her own strengths, her own worries, her own dreams. As I travel around the world and meet with young people from all types of backgrounds, I see some kids brimming with confidence and others who are afraid to raise their hand to even ask a question. I've met students who already have a shelf full of medals and trophies, and those who seem to shrink from their accomplishments to avoid attention or embarrassment. I've met kids ready to embrace their future and those who feel like they have no future at all.

We need to change this for them and for ourselves. Each of us can use the guidance of someone who's been down the road before—and who can help us see the possibilities in front of us. We need someone who can push back on the voices telling us we're not good enough, we're not ready or just plain no.

I was a girl who sometimes heard no, but I learned to disregard the naysayers and seek out the encouragement that got me to yes. I had a mother who pushed me, a father and a big brother who let me know I was beautiful, and an extended family and friends who were proud of me. This support set me on the path to be the professional, wife, mother and First Lady I am today.

When the first issue of ESSENCE came out, in 1970, we had one Black woman in Congress. Now we have 14. We have had Black women serve as secretary of state, ambassador to the United Nations and president of an Ivy League school. Last year we achieved another first as a Black woman became CEO of a Fortune 500 company. Black women have been crowned Miss America and American Idol; we've walked away with a Best Actress Oscar and a Nobel Prize for literature, and two sisters have Grand-Slammed their way through the tennis world.

We've come so far in 40 years, and yet there's still so much untapped potential within us. I can't wait to see what we'll do in the next 40. And if somewhere along the way we need a reminder of who we are or what we can be, we'll know where to turn. ESSENCE will reach out to us, pull us up, and show us that yes, we are beautiful; yes, we are smart; yes, we are fearless. We deserve it, and now we need to believe it.

MICHELLE OBAMA

This article first appeared in the September 2010 issue of ESSENCE.

> *Yes, we are beautiful; yes, we are smart; yes, we are fearless. We deserve it, and now we need to believe it."*
> —MICHELLE OBAMA

MAY 7, 2010, *Washington, D.C.*
The First Lady embracing guests
during a Mother's Day Tea in the State
Dining Room of the White House.

JANUARY 20, 2009, *Washington, D.C.*
President Obama and the First Lady (in Isabel Toledo)
at their Inaugural Parade.

JANUARY 21, 2013, *Washington, D.C.*
The First Lady (in Jason Wu) alongside the President
at the Commander in Chief's Ball.

SEPTEMBER 19, 2011, *New York City*
The Obamas arriving in New York, where the President
will attend the United Nations General Assembly.
Mrs. Obama is wearing a Duro Olowu dress.

OCTOBER 8, 2014, *Washington, D.C.*
The First Lady viewing a display of her dresses in the White House during the Fashion Education Workshop.

We need someone who can push back on the voices telling us we're not good enough." —MICHELLE OBAMA

JUNE 14, 2011, *Berkeley, CA*
Mrs. Obama waits to be introduced at
an event at the Claremont Club & Spa.

MAY 15, 2011, *College Park, GA*
FLOTUS delivering the commencement
address for Spelman College, at the
Georgia International Convention Center,
where she received an honorary degree.

OCTOBER 28, 2013, *Washington, D.C.*
An energetic First Lady during filming for the Animal Planet's *Puppy Bowl.*

JULY 18, 2012, *Birmingham, AL*
Mrs. Obama talking to children attending Camp Noah at the McAlpine Park Recreation Center.

> *I was a girl who sometimes heard no, but I learned to disregard the naysayers and seek out the encouragement that got me to yes."*
> —MICHELLE OBAMA

APRIL 4, 2013, *Washington, D.C.*
The First Lady planting vegetables
with students from across the nation
in the White House Kitchen Garden.

JULY 15, 2011, *Washington, D.C.*
The First Lady shows off her double Dutch skills during
taping for the Presidential Active Lifestyle Award
challenge and Nickelodeon's Worldwide Day of Play.

NOVEMBER 28, 2012, *Washington, D.C.*
The First Lady bonding with children of
military families during a holiday press event.

MARCH 21, 2015, *Siem Reap, Cambodia*
First Lady Obama hugging students during a Let
Girls Learn initiative.

APRIL 4, 2011, *Washington, D.C.*
Dr. Jill Biden and the First Lady striking a pose for
a Joining Forces public-service announcement.

DECEMBER 19, 2013, *Washington, D.C.*
Mrs. Obama greets service members after a
Toys for Tots event.

JANUARY 17, 2013, *Washington, D.C.*
The President singing "Happy Birthday" to his wife after an inaugural brunch at the White House.

— ○ REFLECTION ○ —

THE WOMAN BESIDE HIM

On January 20, 2009, Michelle LaVaughn Robinson Obama will become the nation's first lady. Her achievement is, in some ways, as remarkable as her husband's, especially when we consider a past in which laws challenged whether female slaves were even women; when Black schoolteachers, dressed to the nines, were dragged out of railway "ladies' cars" in a Jim Crow South, where signs distinguished colored bathrooms from White "ladies' rooms." Of course, Michelle Obama was not elected to her first lady position, but this doesn't mean that she hasn't earned it. Back when her husband first launched his campaign, many of us began to take him seriously only after we saw and heard Michelle. That Barack Obama would choose for his life partner a nearly six-foot-tall, incredibly smart, loquacious lioness of a woman told us virtually all we needed to know about his fundamental character—and the way he felt about us.

We know a good deal about her, too, because she has chosen to tell us about her life as well as his, about their courtship and career choices, and about their marriage and children. In addition to convincing us about the virtues of Barack as an agent of change, Michelle has been startlingly frank about her frustrations: doing double duty as a professional and mother during the years of his campaign absences, his domestic shortcomings and her determination to maintain a normal life for their daughters, Malia, 10, and Sasha, 7.

Such revelations are all the more remarkable in light of our historical reticence to expose our personal selves, to take down the shields that keep us from being made vulnerable or ashamed. Although Ms. Obama has been criticized in some quarters for her public airing of private matters, her decision to allow us to listen in on the personal negotiations that have produced a remarkable, loving, twenty-first-century partnership and two breathtaking daughters may be as valuable to us as any policy decision coming from the chief executive's office.

Speaking of criticism, Michelle certainly received her fair share of it on the campaign trail. She is not the kind of Black woman who sits well with everyone. Known as a fierce mother, she has put us on notice that we may borrow her husband, but we cannot have him. He belongs to Malia and Sasha. Michelle is thankful for her Ivy League privileges, but most of her appreciation is reserved for her mother and late father. This country, she seems to say, must earn our gratitude. Indeed, the most controversial aspect of our first lady is her vision. While Barack is publicly willing to forgive the country for its sins, I suspect Michelle is not so sure. She is the one who has been pounding the message about an America that is still divided, that ignores the truly bereft. The most consistent image she evoked in her speeches during the campaign was that of a young girl she met in South Carolina. In *Michelle: A Biography*, by Liza Mundy, the story is recounted. "She knows," said Michelle, "that if she or her family gets sick, she doesn't have access to a primary-care doctor. She's going to be sitting in some ER for hours on end. She knows that her parents' work situation is hit or miss. They don't know what's going to happen day to day. She knows that." Michelle continued, "But you know what she also knows? That she's so much better than this nation's limited expectations of her. And all she has is hope.... You know how I know so much about that little girl? Because she's me. I was not supwosed to be here."

Michelle Obama has been pilloried for bringing an edge to a campaign that stressed unity and reconciliation. She is reminiscent of those figures in our history who have dared to disturb the consensus, who remind us that alongside the ascent of the few is the suffering of the many. The late nineteenth century was another era of tremendous gains for Blacks: William Monroe Trotter was Harvard's first Black Phi Beta Kappa; unprecedented political appointments were granted by the William McKinley administration; opportunities were being sought for women; and an influx of philanthropic financial support flowed to Black institutions. But it was also during this period that the number of lynchings reached new heights and ghettos congealed to choke off opportunities for generations to come. Michelle Obama reminds us that this country is capable of fomenting change even while simultaneously perpetuating cruel inequalities. One suspects that she is not going to let this vision go—and it will be left to us not to allow her to be isolated or mischaracterized by her critics as the angry female interloper who besmirches her husband's postracial presidency. For Michelle Obama, our first first lady who makes us feel that we are supposed to be here, it is the least we can do.

PAULA GIDDINGS

This article first appeared in the January 2009 issue of ESSENCE.

> *Each of us can use the guidance of someone who's been down the road before— and who can help us see the possibilities in front of us."*
> —MICHELLE OBAMA

JUNE 18, 2012, *Chicago*
The First Lady reacting to Laura Jarrett
and Tony Balkissoon reciting vows during
their wedding at Valerie Jarrett's home.

I want to help young people see their potential, to be confident in using their voices, to own the power of their experiences."
—MICHELLE OBAMA

NOVEMBER 24, 2009, *Washington, D.C.*
The First Lady enjoying the entertainment portion of the State Dinner for Prime Minister Manmohan Singh of India and his wife.

JUNE 24, 2016, *Washington, D.C.*
First Lady Michelle Obama and Oprah Winfrey
sharing a laugh during the White House
Summit on the United State of Women.

MARCH 27, 2015, *Washington, D.C.*
The Obamas share a snuggle before
videotaping for the 2015 World Expo.

SEPTEMBER 27, 2014, *Washington, D.C.*
The First Lady watching her husband speak at the Congressional Black Caucus Foundation's 44th Annual Legislative Conference Phoenix Awards Dinner.

MARCH 20, 2015, *Kyoto, Japan*
The First Lady, along with senior monk Eigen Onishi, enjoying tea with Caroline Kennedy, U.S. Ambassador to Japan, at the Kiyomizu-dera Buddhist temple.

"We can take comfort in how far we've come and have confidence in where we're headed."

—MICHELLE OBAMA

JUNE 13, 2014, *Cannon Ball, ND*
First Lady Obama gleaming in a shawl presented to her by Tribe Chairman Dave Archambault II and Mrs. Nicole Archambault during the Cannon Ball Flag Day Celebration.

JULY 18, 2014, *Washington, D.C.*
Joined by the cast of Disney's *The Lion King,* Mrs.
Obama is all smiles after their performance at the
Kids' State Dinner.

APRIL 28, 2015, *Washington, D.C.*
First Lady Obama and First Lady Akie Abe of
Japan are welcomed by Bo and Sunny.

NOVEMBER 7, 2010, *Mumbai, India*
The First Lady dancing with students during a
Diwali candle lighting and performance.

JANUARY 12, 2016, *Washington, D.C.*
First Lady Obama waving as she takes her seat in
the gallery for President Obama's final State of
the Union address to a Joint Session of Congress.

When you've had some success, it's not enough to just sit back and enjoy it."
—MICHELLE OBAMA

MAY 27, 2014, *Washington, D.C.*
ESSENCE Editor-in-Chief Vanessa De
Luca laughing with the First Lady during
an interview for ESSENCE magazine.

OCTOBER 27, 2013, *Washington, D.C.*
The President and First Lady walk with daughters Malia and Sasha through Lafayette Park to attend service at St. John's Church.

CHAPTER THREE
THE FIRST FAMILY

The Obamas represent the quintessential
American success story but have never been
pretentious. Their love for one another is palpable,
and for two terms they opened the doors of the
White House, making us feel like extended kin.

FEBRUARY 24, 2009, *Washington, D.C.*
The First Lady beside her mother, Marian Robinson,
while being photographed in the White House for
our May 2009 ESSENCE cover.

◦ ESSAY ◦

FOUR YEARS IN THE WHITE HOUSE

Grandma in Chief Mrs. Marian Robinson shares cherished moments and reflects on the enduring values that keep the First Family centered as they work to take our nation forward

In September I sat with my son-in-law and my two granddaughters at the White House as we watched my daughter, Michelle, give her speech at the Democratic National Convention. I could tell that she was having a real impact on everyone in that arena down in Charlotte, North Carolina—and I know she sure did with those of us who know her best.

Watching her that night was one of those moments from the last four years that I'll never forget. But to be honest with you, I can't say I was surprised to see my daughter up there making such an impression. From my perspective as a mom and a grandma here in the White House, I see her honesty and strength every day. I see how much she loves her girls and her husband. And I see how hard she and Barack are working to make things better for folks across the country.

Now I know this might sound crazy, but even though I've been living in the White House for the past couple of years, I've got to admit that there are a few things I still miss—like that little bitty house I lived in for decades, and many of my friends and family back in Chicago. But after Barack was elected President and Michelle asked me to move with them to Washington, I said yes because I knew I'd be worrying about them if I was back in Chicago anyway. I just hoped I could be helpful.

You see, my job here is the easiest one of all: I just get to be Grandma. One of my biggest blessings is getting to see my granddaughters grow up before my eyes. I go to all their school plays and sports games; I'll answer their questions, and like any grandparent, I try to make myself scarce when their friends are around.

I'm also thankful to be able to be there for Michelle, as well. She'll ask about parenting, about how her dad and I made decisions when she and her older brother, Craig, were growing up. I just tell it to her straight: There's no textbook that tells you how to be a good parent. The truth is, most of the time you don't really know what to do. You just try to do your best.

We didn't have much when the kids were growing up. My husband, Fraser, worked for the city water plant, and I was a stay-at-home mom for most of their childhood. Like most families, ours went through plenty of ups and downs, but Fraser and I tried to show our kids that when you fall you have to get right back up.

We'd tell them that everybody goes through trials and tribulations, and the people who succeed are the ones who say, "Okay, that's just a snag," and keep on going. I guess that's just the way my husband and I lived.

We also made sure they understood that nothing was more important than their education. While we always knew that a good education started with us as parents at home, we also made sure they were studying hard in school and dreaming big things for themselves. I always told them, "It's not *if* you go to college, but *when* you go to college." And when they'd finally made it there, Fraser and I were proud to keep doing our part to help them continue their studies. Every semester, my husband paid our share of Craig's and Michelle's college tuition, making sure that it wasn't late. We had to take out loans to do it, but we didn't tell them that at the time. We just wanted our children to understand that a good education was their ticket to a better life, a chance to have more and be more than their parents ever dreamed. And so we did everything we could to support them.

Today when I look at Michelle and Craig—a big-time college basketball coach—I feel like maybe, just maybe, Fraser and I got something right. We didn't do anything special. But I see the adults our kids have become and I can't help but smile a little bit. With Michelle, I see how whatever's in front of her, she'll throw her whole heart into it. Whether she's helping kids learn how to eat healthy foods and exercise, supporting our military families or inspiring young people to pursue their dreams, Michelle will always give 110 percent. And if she hits a snag, that's when she gives 120 percent.

Barack is the same way. I often marvel that the two of them found each other in the first place, because they're so similar in so many ways. They both work so hard, they're both so smart, they love each other so much, and they do whatever they can to make the world around them just a little bit better. I'm always impressed by how Barack deals with all these weighty matters, but he never lets them weigh him down. He'll stay up late, reading that big book of papers. He'll get up early and go off to his office for a day full of tough decisions and complicated issues that I'd never wish upon anyone.

JUNE 17, 2015, *Milan, Italy*
The First Lady arrives with daughters
Malia and Sasha and her mother,
Mrs. Robinson, at Malpensa Airport.

JUNE 28, 2016, *Marrakesh, Morocco*
From left to right: Princess Lalla Hasna, Mrs. Robinson, Malia, Sasha, U.S. First Lady Michelle Obama, Princesses Lalla Salma, Lalla Meryem, and Lalla Asma attend an iftar dinner (Ramadan meal) offered by Morocco's King Mohammed VI.

DECEMBER 3, 2015, *Washington, D.C.*
Malia, Sasha, Mrs. Robinson, the First Lady and the President attending the national Christmas tree lighting ceremony at the White House.

MARCH 7, 2015, *Selma, AL*
The President and First Lady joining hands with Representative John Lewis (center) as they lead the walk across the historic Edmund Pettus Bridge to commemorate the 50th Anniversary of Bloody Sunday and the Selma to Montgomery civil rights marches. Malia, Sasha and the girls' grandmother, Mrs. Robinson, stand alongside them.

"We also made sure they understood that nothing was more important than their education."

—MARIAN ROBINSON

> **They [Malia and Sasha] are old enough to have their own ideas and surprise you with the maturity of their insights."**
>
> —PRESIDENT OBAMA

SEPTEMBER 22, 2015, *Camp Springs, MD*
The Obama and Biden families greeting Pope
Francis as he arrives in the United States for
the first time at Joint Base Andrews.

> ## *One of my biggest blessings is getting to see my granddaughters grow up before my eyes."*
> **—MARIAN ROBINSON**

I admire how hard Barack works. And I know that he does it because he wants to make sure that this country is still a place where you can make it if you try. He wants to make sure that a college education is affordable and attainable so that all parents can encourage their kids to reach for it, just like Fraser and I did. He wants to make sure that moms and dads can provide for their families, and folks my age can retire with dignity and security. And he wants every child to believe that they can achieve their dreams, no matter where they come from, what they look like or how much money their parents make. That's what makes him work so hard. I've seen it from him and I've heard it from him. And that's why I'll be voting for him in November, and I hope you do, too.

What amazes me the most, though, is that Barack still makes time for family dinner almost every night. He's still calling out plays from the sideline for Sasha's basketball team. He's talking the girls through their days, helping them with their homework, and laughing and joking with them every single day.

So whether it's as parents or as professionals, Michelle and Barack both truly believe the words that Michelle said in her big speech: "When you've worked hard, and done well, and walked through that doorway of opportunity, you do not slam it shut behind you. You reach back, and you give other folks the same chances that helped you succeed."

That's the way Fraser and I and so many people of our generation lived every day. And really, that's been the biggest highlight of this whole White House experience for me: knowing that Michelle and Barack are living out those values—not only as First Lady and President, but as Mom and Dad.

MARIAN ROBINSON

This article first appeared in the November 2012 issue of ESSENCE.

JULY 17, 2011, *Washington, D.C.*
The First Family intently watching the World Cup
soccer match between the United States and
Japan from the Treaty Room in the White House.

AUGUST 23, 2015, *Washington, D.C.*
President Obama and older daughter Malia
return to the White House after the First
Family's annual vacation in Martha's Vineyard.

AUGUST 14, 2010, *Panama City Beach, FL*
President and First Lady Obama happily
giving daughter Sasha a high five after she
scores a hole in one.

I see how hard she and Barack are working to make things better for folks across the country."
—MARIAN ROBINSON

92

MARCH 31, 2013, *Washington, D.C.*
The First Family strolling to attend an
Easter service at St. John's Church.

93

JUNE 2, 2007, *Concord, NH*
Sasha and Malia enjoying swing time. (This photo,
which includes the Obama daughters' portrait, was
published in the 2008 Family issue of *Real Simple.*)

SWINGING ALONG THE CAMPAIGN TRAIL

This photo was taken last summer in New Hampshire, when the girls were on a trip with Michelle and their grandmother doing some campaigning and kicking off the state chapter of Women for Obama, our campaign's organizing group for women across the country. I couldn't make the trip, because I was campaigning elsewhere, but I know they went to some fairs and festivals, and at some point during the day they ended up getting their faces painted—just experiencing all the joys of summer. I remember Michelle telling me that along the way the girls had some ice cream, cotton candy, and ice cream again, so at least I knew that they were having fun. And because Michelle and I make it a point to limit the girls' participation on the campaign trail, to let kids be kids and let them stay focused on their lives—school, camp, sleepovers, soccer games—being on the trail this day was more of an adventure for them than a chore.

The first thing I notice when I look at this photo is how much they've grown in just a year's time. Malia (on the right) is probably about six inches taller now! On the one hand, I think it captures all the joys that they experience in their childhood. But it also makes me a bit wistful, because even though Michelle and I do everything we can to have the family together on the campaign trail, there are moments I miss. The photo really captures the fact that they are a pair of happy girls. That's a good feeling when I have to be away so much.

And the photo proves that this is just a wonderful age. Sasha (left) is seven, and Malia turned 10 on the Fourth of July. They're at the age where they can look after themselves, set their own alarms, get themselves dressed, and even fix themselves breakfast. We're watching them grow more independent, but they still have that enthusiasm for everything, including their parents, that you worry may vanish when they get to high school. They're old enough to have their own ideas and surprise you with their humor and the maturity of their insights, but they're still young enough to need you. And as a parent, sometimes you need that.

The thing that we really try to instill in them is the Golden Rule. Michelle and I have told them over and over, just treat people the way you'd like to be treated. And we're so blessed that they've ended up being thoughtful, kind children. The other thing we try to teach them is the value of working hard and doing your best. I want them to understand that they're not going to be excellent at everything right away, but the more they try, the more they'll improve.

And I love this photo because it captures just how much they love one another and enjoy each other's company. Sasha is a little more the imp of the two—she always hopes and tries to get a little more attention and pushes the envelope a bit more, like younger siblings usually do. But Malia puts up with it; she's one of the most patient people I know. She's just wise beyond her years. She's usually the one who makes sure that they're responsible; that they put the toys away after they play; that they stop after eating a certain amount of candy. As they've gotten older, they get along very well. They've come to enjoy each other's company in a way that makes you feel good as a parent.

SENATOR BARACK OBAMA
(as told to Rachel Hardage)

This article first appeared in the Fall 2008 edition of *Real Simple*.

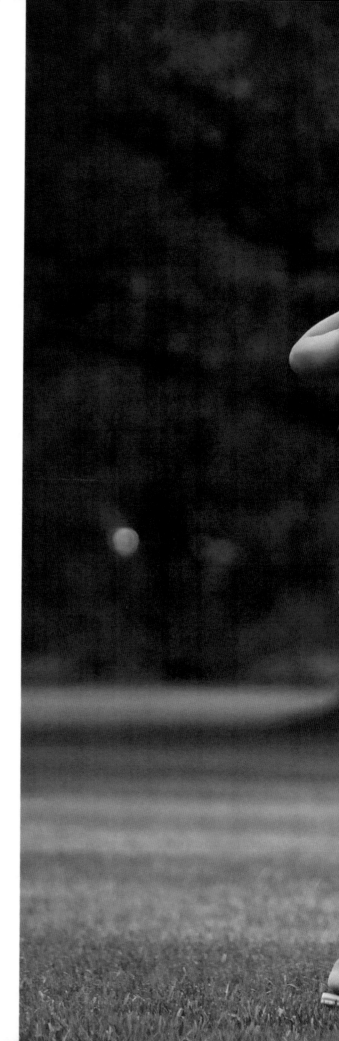

The thing that we really try to instill in them is the Golden Rule. Michelle and I have told them over and over, just treat people the way you'd like to be treated. And we're so blessed that they've ended up being thoughtful, kind children."

—PRESIDENT OBAMA

SEPTEMBER 15, 2009, *Washington, D.C.*
President Obama receives a warm welcome
from daughters Sasha and Malia and dog Bo
on the South Lawn of the White House.

"
While we always knew that a good education started with us as parents at home, we also made sure they were studying hard in school and dreaming big things for themselves."
—MARIAN ROBINSON

JUNE 21, 2011, *Johannesburg, South Africa*
Nelson Mandela with the First Lady and daughters
Malia and Sasha at his Johannesburg home.

APRIL 25, 2011, *Washington, D.C.*
Sasha and Malia reading a book to children
during the annual Easter egg roll on the
South Lawn of the White House.

> *We just wanted our children to understand that a good education was their ticket to a better life, a chance to have more and be more than their parents ever dreamed."*
> —MARIAN ROBINSON

JUNE 19, 2008, *Chicago*
Sasha and Malia being photographed
in their home for the ESSENCE
September 2008 cover.

SEPTEMBER 4, 2012, *Washington, D.C.*
President Obama flanked by Malia and Sasha
while watching the First Lady deliver her speech
at the Democratic National Convention.

JANUARY 21, 2013, *Washington, D.C.*
Sasha and Malia sneaking in a playful selfie
during the Presidential Inaugural Parade.

NOVEMBER 25, 2015, *Washington, D.C.*
Sasha and Malia watching as President Obama
pardons the National Thanksgiving Turkey
in the Rose Garden of the White House.

JUNE 16, 2015, *London, England*
Sasha walking along Downing Street.

JUNE 16, 2015, *London, England*
Malia during a London visit.

ET made for you by local
growers and producers

Catering & E

We can bring our truck, "B
or one of our carts to your
party, picnic, fiesta, or corp

Ask us for more info
pleasantpops.com/c

NOVEMBER 28, 2015, *Washington, D.C.*
President Obama buying ice cream for
Malia and Sasha at Pleasant Pops during
Small Business Saturday.

JANUARY 20, 2009, *Washington, D.C.*
President Obama takes the oath of office from Chief Justice John Roberts as First Lady Obama holds the Lincoln Bible and daughters Malia and Sasha watch at the U.S. Capitol.

JULY 16, 2012, *Washington, D.C.*
Kiss Cam! The President grabs a smooch from the First Lady during a basketball game at the Verizon Center.

AUGUST 15, 2012, *Davenport, IA*
The President holds hands with the First Lady
after she introduces him at a campaign event.

ESSENCE TIME INC. BOOKS

EDITOR-IN-CHIEF Vanessa K. De Luca
EXECUTIVE EDITOR Jacklyn Monk
EDITORIAL PROJECTS DIRECTOR Patrik Henry Bass

FROM THE EDITORS OF ESSENCE
THE OBAMAS: THE WHITE HOUSE YEARS
EDITOR Patrik Henry Bass
DESIGN DIRECTOR Pinda D. Romain
PHOTO EDITOR Patricia Cadley
ART DIRECTOR Elsa Mehary
PRODUCTION MANAGER Dawn Abbott
REPORTER/RESEARCHER Bridgette Bartlett Royall
COPY EDITOR Pamela Grossman
WRITERS Paula Giddings, Rachel Hardage, Barack Obama, Michelle Obama, Marian Robinson

PUBLISHER Margot Schupf
ASSOCIATE PUBLISHER Allison Devlin
VICE PRESIDENT, FINANCE Terri Lombardi
VICE PRESIDENT, MARKETING Jeremy Biloon
EXECUTIVE DIRECTOR, MARKETING SERVICES Carol Pittard
DIRECTOR, BRAND MARKETING Jean Kennedy
FINANCE DIRECTOR Kevin Harrington
SALES DIRECTOR Christi Crowley
ASSISTANT GENERAL COUNSEL Andrew Goldberg
ASSISTANT DIRECTOR, PRODUCTION Susan Chodakiewicz
SENIOR MANAGER, CATEGORY MARKETING Bryan Christian
BRAND MANAGER Katherine Barnet
ASSOCIATE PROJECT MANAGER & PRODUCTION Anna Riego
ASSOCIATE PREPRESS MANAGER Alex Voznesenskiy

EDITORIAL DIRECTOR Kostya Kennedy
CREATIVE DIRECTOR Gary Stewart
DIRECTOR OF PHOTOGRAPHY Christina Lieberman
EDITORIAL OPERATIONS DIRECTOR Jamie Roth Major
SENIOR EDITOR Alyssa Smith
ASSISTANT ART DIRECTOR Anne-Michelle Gallero
COPY CHIEF Rina Bander
ASSISTANT MANAGING EDITOR Gina Scauzillo
ASSISTANT EDITOR Courtney Mifsud

SPECIAL THANKS Brad Beatson, Nicole Fisher, Kristina Jutzi, Seniqua Koger, Kate Roncinske

ESSENCE

THE OBAMAS: THE WHITE HOUSE YEARS
PHOTO CREDITS

APRIL 5, 2015, *Washington, D.C.*
President Barack Obama, First Lady Michelle Obama, and daughters Malia and Sasha pose for a family portrait with Bo and Sunny in the Rose Garden of the White House on Easter Sunday.

JANUARY 21, 2013, *Washington, D.C.*
President Barack Obama dances with First Lady
Michelle Obama at the Commander-in-Chief Ball
following his second-term inauguration earlier that day.

Made in the USA
Lexington, KY
22 January 2017